MW01129981

VIETNAM PHOTOGRAPHS
FROM NORTH CAROLINA VETERANS

VIETNAM PHOTOGRAPHS FROM NORTH CAROLINA VETERANS

The Memories They Brought Home

MARTIN TUCKER

THE
History
PRESS

Published by The History Press
Charleston, SC
www.historypress.com

Copyright © 2019 by Martin Tucker
All rights reserved

First published 2019

ISBN 9781540240040

Library of Congress Control Number: 2019939737

This book is dedicated to my two uncles who served in World War II; my uncle who served in Korea; my nephew, a Citadel graduate and U.S. Navy veteran; and my father, an "old salt" who sailed the North Atlantic as a gunner's mate in World War II.

Your willingness to step up to the call set an example for us all.

CONTENTS

SILENT MEMORIES

PHOTOGRAPHS OF VIETNAM

THE IMPORTANT THING TO REMEMBER about looking at photographs is that they always have the power to evoke memories, especially memories of times once forgotten, of faces from long ago and of places once visited. For Vietnam veterans, the memories of their war experiences are sometimes accompanied by fear and anguish, and they have buried those thoughts so deep that no one can penetrate the depth of their wounds. Silence becomes not only their language of choice but also a bond between brothers who fought side by side and vowed to never mention the horrors they witnessed. Photographs are profound images that can spark the most intimate details of survival for soldiers. They become words when the scenes are indescribable and for those of us who were not there in Vietnam. The photographs become the beginning of stories never told. Photographs help veterans break their silences and travel back to that place that turned boys into men.

Perhaps photographs are all we need to complete the story of Vietnam, for without them we only have scattered memories that desperately need to attach themselves to something that once made us whole. For Vietnam veterans, who perhaps never possessed the voice to speak about the time in Vietnam, these photos have the power to speak for them.

—SHARON RAYNOR, PhD
Professor of English
Project Director, The Silence of War and
Breaking the Silence: The Unspoken Brotherhood of Vietnam Veterans

MY PAST

MOST WOULD AGREE **that to** have a happy life we must minimize our regrets, focus on the future, but never completely forget the past. The opening of the touring exhibit of "A Thousand Words: Photographs by Vietnam Veterans" at the North Carolina Museum of History in Raleigh will put my past in front of me once again. I first experienced these powerful images at a one-time exhibit at the Sawtooth Center in Winston-Salem in 2003. This "past" for me was my Vietnam experience, where straight out of high school (1967) I enlisted in the Navy. By January 1968, I was in-country heading for a little hamlet south of Saigon called Mey Tuo.

I was joining a group of extraordinary young men. The unit was a Navy special warfare small boat unit not seen in action since the Civil War. Union river runners, the earlier prototype, had proved very successful, and now the Navy had once again opted for riverine warfare. The scope of our mission was to search the many junks, sampans and water taxis plying the Mekong Delta. We were looking for arms and supplies that the Viet Cong desperately needed. Most of the locals were going about their lives as usual and accepted the Americans' daily intrusion as part of life. Looking back, it was these day patrols—with the children smiling, the peasant women with their teeth blackened by betel nuts and the old men tending their nets—that offered a true glimpse into life along the Mekong Delta. I came to appreciate the people of Vietnam. I also became vigilant to ambush during night operations in tiny jungle-encroaching canals and to intercede the movement of the Viet Cong. These canals were "Charlie's" home, and pursuing him would often have dire consequences, putting us in harm's way, where night could erupt with tracers and flying metal. And it would be years before I ever heard the words, "Welcome home brother," which of course represent a sort of acceptance.

The pictures I took represent both sides of Vietnam, but all represent a past that transcends the miles, years, hurt and pain of Vietnam. I would like to think that these photos are a rare opportunity to experience that past and to honor the living and the dead.

—David M. Prevette
U.S. Navy, 1968

MY CAMERA

As a Team Leader with G Company Rangers, I was issued a camera to photograph objects with potential for intelligence use. The camera was an Olympus Pen EES-2 35mm half-frame and was fairly compact by late '60s and early '70s standards, but it was certainly not a tiny, elaborate, James Bond–style device. I was issued black-and-white film with thirty-six-picture capability, and being a half-frame camera, it would yield seventy-two exposures. We took pictures of any object or place that had intelligence value, like structures, improved trails, points of regular river crossings and any other objects that were of interest. I would submit the film to the S-2 shop (Intel) for development, but I soon learned that I rarely got any of the exposures back. I started buying my own film at the PX, switched to color and then would submit any Intel-worthy negatives to S-2 once I got them back from the PX, where they were developed.

I took far more pictures of the team members on mission than I ever did for Intel purposes. When we were on a reconnaissance mission (Long Range Reconnaissance Patrols, or LRRP), which most of them were, we often monitored trails or river crossings for enemy use. Such surveillance would often last for several days, making no sound and rotating "watch" positions and radio duty while others on the six-man team would nap or read paperback books that were brought along. Many of our missions involved roving reconnaissance each day in an attempt to cover as much territory as possible in our assigned grid, and there were few opportunities for photos while moving, as the potential for enemy contact increased while moving. But there was often time for taking pictures during missions that lasted four to six days. We could not be resupplied by helicopters, as were line infantry units, because it would compromise our location to the enemy. With only six men on a team, we avoided enemy contact when possible. No noise, no talking above a whisper and no smoking or cooking rations was allowed. But the faint *click* of the camera when taking pictures was almost undetectable to the ear. When we were in our company area and off mission, I used a Minolta 35mm camera I bought at the PX that took better-quality pictures but was too large to be carried in the field.

Photos are great reminders of the guys, the views and experiences of Vietnam and are more important to me now than when they were originally taken. When attending our reunions, many of the guys will bring their old photos to share memories.

I still have my issued camera!

—AL STEWART
U.S. Army, 1970–73

MY INSPIRATION

GROWING UP IN WINSTON-SALEM, NORTH CAROLINA, I would see *National Geographic* magazines at school and read them from cover to cover. All the pictures of things and places I'd never seen before were very interesting to me. My visual trips through *National Geographic* magazines inspired me to take pictures of the places I traveled to while in the military. In this book you'll see some of those pictures.

—JOSEPH ANTHONY
U.S. Marine Corps, Scout Dogs
1968

ACKNOWLEDGEMENTS

THE ORIGINAL PROJECT COMMITTEE MEMBERS were Steve Acesta (U.S. Coast Guard, Ret.), Brian Cox, Diana Greene (oral historian), Carolyn Lukason, Nancy Pitkin, George Schober (U.S. Marine Corps Vietnam veteran), Vicki Schober, Sara Spendiff and Robin Underhill. Without their selfless work, the exhibit would not have been possible. It's never easy to approach businesses and corporations for donations, but every one of the companies contacted contributed with monetary and in-kind assistance. Small businesses—including mom and pop restaurants, hair salons, realtors, car washes, motorcycle shops and landscapers—showed their appreciation to the veterans. The Winston-Salem/Forsyth County Arts Council provided the Milton Rhodes Gallery in the Sawtooth building for the first exhibit. The regional and national news media provided coverage that pushed the traveling show out into communities up and down the East Coast. The North Carolina Humanities Council provided grant assistance. The Southeastern Center for Contemporary Art donated wooden crates so the exhibit could travel. The North Carolina Helicopter Pilots Association displayed a Huey helicopter for school visits. And a special thanks goes out to the numerous private citizens who chose to support a generation of veterans.

But the most valuable contribution of all is from the Vietnam veterans who opened up those dusty shoeboxes and photo albums and shared their experiences with us. Without their courage to revisit their past, this book would not be possible.

Special note: The majority of the captions are veterans' quotes. These remain verbatim. All photographs are from the veterans' personal collections and are used with permission.

INTRODUCTION

Winston-Salem, North Carolina
March 2005

A
S I LOOK AROUND MY OFFICE at the Sawtooth School for Visual Art, I find it hard to believe that not too long ago, boxes of photographs surrounded me. Not just a few boxes, but boxes stacked from the floor to the ceiling. The boxes contained four thousand photographs.

It began as an idea to give my black-and-white photography students something different to print in the darkroom. We'd post a few flyers around the Triad asking Vietnam veterans to loan us any black-and-white negatives they might still have from their tours, and then my students would make enlargements from them. We'd give the veterans a nice print for participating and tack the photos on the bulletin board, and hopefully the students would get a history lesson in the bargain. And that would be the end of it.

As a Vietnam-era vet myself, I called the local veterans organizations and asked if I could come in and make a short pitch. "If you have any negatives and could loan them to us, I promise we'll take good care of them. You can even come over and watch your photograph come up in the developing tray." The posters, along with the meetings, must have gotten the word out, as a few weeks later the phone started to ring. The veterans said they didn't have any negatives, but they had photographs. Small 3x5 color and black-and-white photographs and Kodacrome slides.

The first vet to offer a photograph was a friend. He was a businessman by day and an avid photographer on the weekends. He'd previously taken the very class whose students I was hoping to enlighten with the negatives. When I mentioned the Vietnam idea to him, he simply said he had a few photographs. I didn't know he was a Vietnam vet. Later, his opinion became very important as photographs began to flood in.

The second vet to come in didn't bring photos. What he brought was a strong curiosity and concern about why I wanted all these pictures. He was a past president of the local chapter of the Vietnam Veterans of America. I told him that I was also a vet and was doing this for the right reasons. He came back three weeks later with five prized photographs and a story of being pinned down in a firefight the first week he was in Vietnam. It left me drained.

I realized that I needed to start keeping a journal of my meetings with the vets. They didn't want to just drop off the photos—they wanted to talk. The ones who came in first had emotional stories that poured out of them. All these years later and their memories, and the strong feelings that came with them, were still just below the surface.

Everyone I talked to about the project knew someone who'd served in Vietnam. A maintenance man in my building lost two brothers over there. A colleague's uncle had gone but had never spoken about it after he returned. He sent his photo album through his niece and would later open up unexpectedly about Vietnam at a family Thanksgiving dinner. Someone mentioned that the owner of a shoeshine shop had been over there. I went to see him, and he simply said, "I was so angry when I came home, I tore them all up." I began to connect the dots from one vet to another. An Iraq vet who was a firefighter in Kernersville said that his barber was in Vietnam. I made three trips to his barbershop before I finally met him. A small American flag and his Honorable Discharge certificate were displayed next to the mirror behind his barber chair. I explained what I was doing, and he said, "I took a lot of pictures." Then he bent over and tapped his artificial leg and said, "But I was medivac'd out and left them all there." He suggested another vet he knew who did have photographs.

As the vets and photos kept coming, I researched and discovered that Vietnam veterans' personal images had never been collected and displayed. I decided to form a committee and put up a formal exhibit of the photographs. We began soliciting for donations to cover the cost of ink, paper and frames. Sawtooth students and volunteers from local middle schools, high schools, colleges and the community came in to scan and digitally repair the old photographs before we printed enlargements. The number one rule was to maintain the integrity of the original.

At about that time I met with a vet from Greensboro who had served as an Army Ranger. He was retired from the Guilford County Sheriff's Department. His wife came along, and we looked through three albums full of photos. He had some very powerful images. When I asked if I could borrow the albums to make digital scans of some of his photos, he wanted to know how long I wanted to keep them. I said about a month, and he replied, "That's OK, if I don't hear from you, I'll hunt you down and kill you." When his wife saw my shocked expression, she said, "Don't mind him, he tells the UPS guy the same thing." (I did get his photos back in a timely manner.) A woman called to say that her mother had passed away and she'd just found all the love letters that her deceased father had sent to her mother when he was in Vietnam. We sat and read them together. Another vet came in with several photos and two original Western Union telegrams that were sent to his parents each time he was wounded in battle. He was still wearing a Purple Heart medallion on a chain around his neck. A Winston-Salem man called to say he had his father's photographs from Vietnam. His father, now deceased, had completed five tours, and he wanted to honor him by loaning us his photos.

After we had secured a location for the exhibit, framed it and were making plans for a reception, a committee member who was a commentator for the local NPR station made a suggestion that forever changed the exhibit. "Why not invite the vets back, let them look at the photos we chose for the exhibit and tape-record their thoughts and comments on their photos?" So, on a Sunday afternoon in May, the quiet, mild-mannered, middle-aged men came back one at a time and remembered. And wept. And began to find closure. Those moving comments—in their own words—became the quotes that now accompany the photographs.

I've had calls from vets in Virginia, South Carolina and Florida and as far away as Washington State. They all have photos and just want to make sure that the story is told fairly and accurately—no hype, no spin. "Just don't make me out to be some hero," they say. How do you take four thousand photographs and tell a soldier's story of what it was like to serve in Vietnam? The key to that question is the "soldier's story." This wasn't intended to be a statement of whether we should have been in Vietnam. It was always about the soldiers in Vietnam—about what they *saw* in Vietnam. We only had room for sixty framed 8x10 photographs in that first exhibit. We scanned more than four hundred as *maybes*. Whenever I got stumped on whether to keep a photo in or not, I asked myself a simple question: "Would a Vietnam vet be able to stand in front of that photograph and say, 'That's exactly the way it was, right there.'" If it passed that test, it stayed in.

The majority of the vets who participated in that project had never spoken about their experiences in Vietnam. Not to their parents, not to their wives and not to their children. They didn't come home to a parade. Wives have told me, "We just don't talk about it." For the first time, those vets have been able to stand in front of those photographs with their children, spouses and parents and say proudly, "That's the way it was. I just never could say it, but those photographs say it for me."

The exhibit became a nationwide tour. More than twenty thousand people viewed it at the Air Zoo Museum in Kalamazoo, Michigan. One thousand people saw it in the first week in small-town Waynesville, North Carolina. And after it was exhibited for a year at the North Carolina Museum of History in Raleigh, the curators said if I ever wanted to give it a permanent home they would like to have it. It was donated to the museum in 2017.

The Comment Books that traveled with the photographs are full of personal reflections about brothers, fathers, sons, uncles and friends who served and never spoke of it. Some lost limbs, some lost their innocence and some lost their lives. The vets write their military branch, company names, locations and dates of service. Family members say, "I just want to see what they went through." Members of the community say, "Thanks for remembering." You can hear a pin drop when high school students see a presentation of it. After all, the boys in those photos were teenagers too. It's taken on a life of its own. It's brought people together and given them an opportunity to understand and thank an entire generation of men and women. And it's opened up a dialogue between husbands and wives, fathers and sons and complete strangers.

The photographs and quotes in this book paint as broad a picture as possible, for the first time, of what eighteen- to twenty-year-old young men from North Carolina experienced in their year away from home (in addition to combat)—and how they chose to document it. But the images speak for Vietnam veterans everywhere. They're showing what they couldn't say.

The project began with seventy dollars in start-up funds and generous donations from the community. But the biggest contribution of all was from the veterans themselves, who chanced revisiting one of the most significant periods of their lives and sharing it with others. This exhibit and book were created for and by them.

Map of South Vietnam, 1966–67. This image is in the public domain, via Wikimedia Commons. It contains material that originally came from the United States Army Center of Military History. https://commons.wikimedia.org.

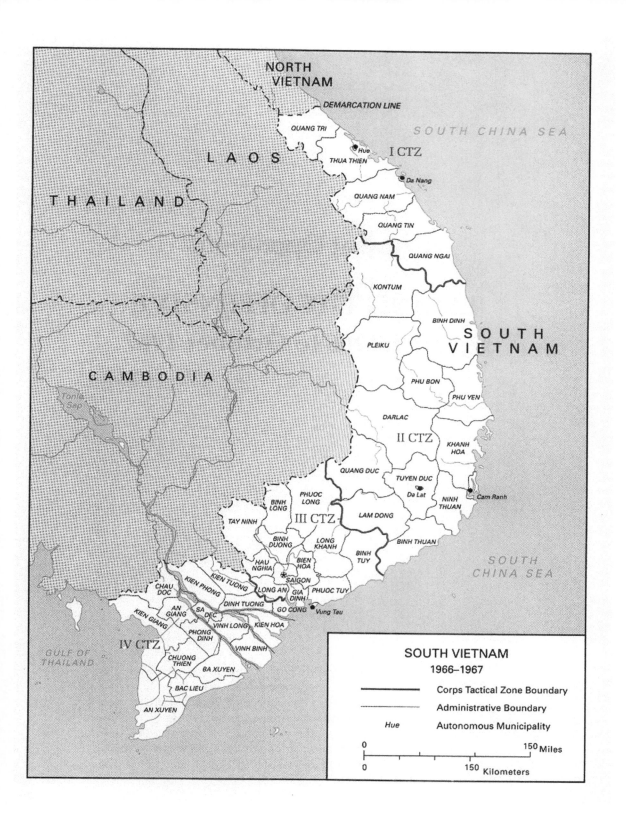

NORTH VIETNAM

DEMARCATION LINE

SOUTH CHINA SEA

LAOS

THAILAND

CAMBODIA

Tonle Sap

QUANG TRI

Hue
THUA THIEN
I CTZ

Da Nang
QUANG NAM

QUANG TIN

QUANG NGAI

KONTUM

BINH DINH

SOUTH
VIETNAM

PLEIKU

PHU BON

PHU YEN

DARLAC

II CTZ

KHANH
HOA

QUANG DUC

TUYEN DUC

Da Lat
NINH
THUAN

Cam Ranh

PHUOC
LONG

BINH
LONG

TAY NINH

III CTZ

LAM DONG

SOUTH
CHINA
SEA

BINH
DUONG

LONG
KHANH

BINH THUAN

HAU
NGHIA

BIEN
HOA

BINH
TUY

CHAU
DOC

KIEN TUONG

KIEN PHONG

SAIGON

LONG AN

GIA
DINH
PHUOC TUY

DINH TUONG

GO CONG

Vung Tau

AN
GIANG

SA
DEC

VINH LONG

KIEN HOA

KIEN GIANG

PHONG
DINH

VINH BINH

GULF OF
THAILAND

IV CTZ

CHUONG
THIEN

BA XUYEN

BAC LIEU

AN XUYEN

SOUTH VIETNAM
1966–1967

—————— Corps Tactical Zone Boundary

- - - - - - - Administrative Boundary

Hue Autonomous Municipality

0   150 Miles

0   150 Kilometers

He had to be pulled out of the mud by rope because he got stuck, and that's the reason he was covered literally head to toe in mud. And he was standing there, and as you can see, he has an attitude. So I took his photograph. I didn't know if he was going to turn around and hit me or whatever, but we all pretty much were upset that we had to cross this river. See, this river would, when the tide would go out, it would drop maybe ten feet, and this silty mud would just suck you up, so you would just have to climb through this mud, and it was really bad. *Robert Karraker, U.S. Army, 1969.*

THE IMAGES

Above When the cameras first came out, they had that shutter speed, 1/1000th of a second, 1/500th of a second. If you had 1/1000th you had something. I just had a 1/500th, and what I was trying to do was stop those blades on those helicopters. So, anyhow, I got all ten of them stopped. In Vietnam, there was helicopters all the time, day and night, twenty-four seven. That's a big formation, ten. Most times they run in fours, six probably. *Andy West, U.S. Army, 1966.*

Opposite, top We were moving from one location in I Corp to another on Route 9. This road went east to west, from the South China Sea to Laos in the northernmost area of South Vietnam, just below the DMZ. I was riding in the back of a truck, and as we passed these guys I raised my camera up and everyone connected with the camera at the same time. The raised "V" symbols were a combined victory-peace gesture; it was a spontaneous moment between comrades. *George Schober, U.S. Marine Corps, 1969.*

Opposite, bottom I think this photograph was taken on Christmas Day of 1969. They brought in two or three helicopters that day. We were being resupplied out in the field. This is just a typical UHIH Huey helicopter. They did bring in hot food, turkey and dressing and cranberry sauce and all that. They tried to be as good to us as they could over there. You can see, there's only one guy wearing a helmet, several of the guys aren't carrying their weapon. It was pretty safe at that point. *Mike Callahan, U.S. Army, 1969.*

26

We were actually setting up surveillance on a river and going to do ambush on a river, hoping to catch some enemy bringing weapons and material down the river in sampans. And we were walking this area of the river and we found a bunker complex—actually it was more like a tunnel complex—and we ended up with just a tremendous weapons cache. There were probably forty machine guns, cases of rifles, 120-millimeter rockets, several mortars, just thousands of mortar rounds, a Singer sewing machine, a foot peddle job I guess they were using to make uniforms with. Communist radios. This NVA flag is in my office now. I have that framed in my office. It was a pretty big find for us. *Al Stewart, U.S. Army, 1971.*

Opposite I'd been there approximately 300 days at that point. It's disturbing to look at it because if you look at the hands we were always filthy. Our fingernails were broken and down into the quick of our fingers. That was up near the Cambodian border. Talk about frightening. Even though they said we didn't go in there, we went in frequently across the border. Of course it was all jungle, so we didn't know. We were never off duty. Being in a war zone, you got to understand, there are different ways to get killed during the different periods of the day. There'd be times where you'd be standing, waiting for the patrol to move up. You'd actually blackout or pass out standing upright; it was the only rest you got. The most valuable thing you see in that picture is the ballpoint pen in my pocket. *Joe Idol, U.S. Army, 1968.*

I flew dust-offs for maybe a couple of weeks, just trying to get pictures. But when this landed here, I had no idea where we were going, and then, this was my old infantry unit, these were my guys. So it really hit me. And the guy who is being brought out here was brought on the helicopter. We took him back to our base hospital. They did surgery on him, stabilized him, and then I flew with him to Saigon. Basically the dust-off was the story at the time, but of course, it expanded. *Robert Karraker, U.S. Army, 1969.*

Da Nang. Waiting on the helo-pad for our birds to take us into the field. *Al Stewart, U.S. Army, 1970.*

Huey helicopters were referred to as "slicks," and this photograph was taken from a slick, out of the South China Sea. We were headed who knows where on some sort of operation. I don't remember anything specific other than there probably would have been six of us on the helicopter getting ready to be put on the ground. What would generally happen is that the little birds would fly around low and try to spot enemy and try to draw fire, and once they spotted enemy, drew fire, Cobra gun ships would come in and fire the area up. Then they would put us on the ground, and we would sweep through the area and see if we could maintain contact with enemy, find out anything or recover bodies. *Al Stewart, U.S. Army, 1971.*

We had went down there, to Bien Hoa, to pick up supplies. We'd go pick up C-rations, and a lot of time pick up pallets of Cokes and stuff for the battery area. I think all these cars here are probably French cars, every one of them. There was a million motorcycles over there, little ol' scooters. It just shows you it was a pretty place. It wasn't a trashy place. I was standing on the back of a five-ton truck and took that picture. After I got my camera, I took it everywhere I went if I could. *Andy West, U.S. Army, 1967.*

It was that "hearts and minds" thing, back in the early stages of Vietnam, so you're out here kind of mingling with the people; you were kind of like a policeman, you might say. These people are getting ready to get into water taxis. In the Mekong Delta that's how they get around. There were no roads. Their roads were all water. So this was a gathering point, a little hamlet where people are coming and getting ready to go to market. In that time, most of the places we'd go to, it was just old people, women, young children. And looking back at this particular picture, I think the striking thing about it is, there's a man. He's getting ready to hand me his ID. Most of these guys were either conscripted by the Vietnamese regular army forces, or they were in hiding or they were active Viet Cong outright or sympathizers. It was rare that you would see men. *David Prevette, U.S. Navy, 1969.*

That ol' guy there was Gilbert Vasquez. He was from San Jose, California. I told him, I said, "If you get out there, Gilbert, I'll take your picture." Gilbert would do about anything, to get in the picture especially. During the monsoons it was warm and wet and messy and it just rained continuously. It's probably about eighteen inches there; it's up to his shorts, well above his knees. It didn't have no place to go. That place was flat. It rained day and night. It didn't quit. *Andy West, U.S. Army, 1965.*

Keith Cunningham was on team Miami, and I was team leader for team Moscow. I'm on the left. The only thing I can think to attribute to the expressions on our face is we're putting on our game face. We're getting ready to go out on a mission, and life changes when you're getting ready to go out. Your mindset changes. One of the most important things about being in the Rangers in the Long Range Reconnaissance Unit was packing for a mission. Everything you took on your mission you carried on your back. We had to have enough ammunition to be able to sustain a 45-minute firefight. I look at these things and I see a two-quart canteen cover. It doesn't have any canteens in it. It has 30-round magazines in it. This one-quart canteen cover, it also carries magazines. All the way around I've got ammunition. I hate to embellish it, but I think we generally carried anywhere from 100 to 110 pounds. *Al Stewart, U.S. Army, 1971.*

This is a scene that you would see in Vietnam with a motorized piece of armory, probably a 105 Howitzer, probably one of the guys who operated it with his shirt off because it was so warm over there. In the foreground is a two-gallon insecticide sprayer. I had a preventive medicine unit. And a simple little two-gallon sprayer was a critical thing to have in each one of the units because they had to spray for cockroaches and fleas around mess halls and various areas. *Gerald Harrison, U.S. Army, 1970.*

Near Pleiku. We ran supply convoys, 50 to 90 trucks from Qhinon (port city) to Central Highlands—Ahn Kay, Pleiku, Bon Son, Cheo Rio and others. Hauled ammo, rations, concertina wire, etc. Vietnamese and Montanyard young people gathered at convoy staging areas and offloading areas looking for handouts and "favors." *Ralph Lee, U.S. Army, 1966.*

Opposite This is an area very close to the old provincial capital of Vietnam, the city of Hue. In the city of Hue they produced ice for the troops. This represents a typical couple of kids on a sampan, and the boat was in an area referred to as Sampan Alley. It was very common to come along and you would see people washing their clothes in the river, then taking the water out of the river and drinking it, using the bathroom in the river and then drinking out of the river. It was incredible how they survived; their intestinal flora must have been something. It was surprising—they were very gentle kids. This one looks like she's seen a lot for her age. I would say that Sampan Alley was a pretty tough place to grow up. *Gerald Harrison, U.S. Army, 1970.*

My last five months on my extension tour I flew as a gunner on a Night Hawk helicopter. We flew from six in the evening until six in the morning. We got shot down. And from the time that we got hit to the time that we crashed, couldn't have been more than about 15 seconds. We were flying real low. Our pilot, a guy named W.O. Osburg, he was getting ready to go home. It was his last flight with Night Hawk in Vietnam. Mr. Osburg flew that helicopter and I think it was skill and luck combined, but we crashed and he nosed into that culvert purely by accident. The next day we came back to recover the helicopter, and of course all I wanted was to take pictures of it. There was a village right there near the area. And they came out, kind of like a train wreck or a car wreck, and everybody wants to look at it. I don't even think I saw those people that day. It was not until I saw the photograph that I said, damn, there's a lot of people watching there. *Al Stewart, U.S. Army, 1972.*

This represents a mad minute of fire around the perimeter of one of the bases. With the cloak of darkness, the enemy felt it had greater opportunity to be concealed, and it was a prime time for attacks to come along the perimeter. It's actually beautiful at night to see all this going off. *Gerald Harrison, U.S. Army, 1970.*

This was Cambodia. A mission that was called Parrot's Beak; it was the first insertion of troops into Cambodia. There was a good-sized river that ran here, and we landed where we thought there was a supply connection for the North Vietnamese. The command group that I was with found the weapons cache. This was a huge complex built into the side of a mountain. There was a hospital there. It was not something that the North Vietnamese were willing to give up easily. We simply had to go in far enough to find out what was going on; in the process, we went from 120 men to 82 that day. It wasn't safe to bring the helicopters back in and take us out. We were just going to have to spend the night. So, we put half of our people down the embankment to the river, to protect us from the back, and the other half of us stayed up on the crest of the river. And I got a call on the radio that said that two gunboats with South Vietnamese troops were making their way up the river. We had something coming. Then, just at dusk, the first of the two gunboats arrived, and they were ARVN, South Vietnamese soldiers. Forty of our people were already dug in on the riverbank, and the ARVNs saw them, thought they were enemy and opened fire. And we lost 23 more. Dead. So, unfortunately, when the ARVNs opened fire on us, we started returning fire, and we couldn't get it stopped. We just couldn't get it stopped. There were 7 of us out of a platoon that was, I think, 22 people. And so, they left, and kind of abandoned us where we were. I took the picture because I wanted some memory of the event that had something positive, and it was the only thing I could find. We stayed another seven days. *Larry Dishon, U.S. Army, 1970.*

Bob Hope, he did the Christmas show. This is in 1966. This was a place called Tent City—it's where we lived, in tents. We were able to get close because I was a military policeman and we were there at the stage, in case something happened. We were there to protect Bob Hope and the other people. There were thousands and thousands of troops, as far as you could see. Army, Navy, Marines. That was a huge gathering, and you kind of had to be on your toes because you could have been hit during one of those shows. Everybody in one spot. *Robert Crutchfield, U.S. Army, 1966.*

This is two of the guys who went to Vietnam with me. We went through dog school down in Fort Benning, Georgia, together. Dink was from the Northeast and Davis was from Ohio. Out of the 17 of the dog hounds that went over there together, there was only three of us who didn't get wounded, and Dink and I were two of them, and there was another fellow too. The group that I went over with, we were such a real close group of guys, like brothers. One get into it, something go wrong, we all in it. That's the way it was. We were just a close-knit group. Real close. *Joe Anthony, U.S. Marine Corps, 1968.*

We'd been in a running firefight with an NVA unit, which was pretty unusual in our area. We mostly faced Viet Cong down there, but that was an NVA trooper that we killed. We were chasing them at that point. We were in basically an irrigation ditch for rice paddies. We never would get up on the rice paddies because the enemy usually mined those things, and there was just no future in that. The man on the left was feeling some apprehension, some fear. Everybody was scared to death that day. That was hard times. *Mike Callahan, U.S. Army, 1970.*

Above The thing that I do remember about the southern part of Vietnam is the beautiful greens, the beautiful blue sky. It's a beautiful country, and then you take this very just idyllic picture—those clouds—and everything, and then, *Oh, wait a minute, what's wrong here?* You got these army troops. When you think about it, these guys are going into harm's way. *David Prevette, U.S. Navy, 1969.*

Opposite, top I had a pilot's license when I went to Vietnam, and my unit was right next to a helicopter unit. So I was friends with a lot of those guys, and they used to take me out flying with them all the time. This Cobra was a primary gunship used in Vietnam for attack purposes. There are two occupants in it. The individual that's in the back is the pilot of the plane. The guy in the front is the gunner, who does the firing of all the guns. It had two primary types of weapons on it. It had rocket pods and what I referred to as a mini gun, which is a motorized Gatling gun that fired 5,000 rounds a minute. It was astounding. *Gerald Harrison, U.S. Army, 1971.*

Opposite, bottom We were waiting on transportation. We were in the northern part of Dong Ha. We were getting ready to get a chopper out. At times you have to just relax, but even by looking like I'm relaxed, you'd still be on edge. Over there, you never know when you were going to get hit or where you were going to get hit from. I'm a different person now. I never want that part of me to come back out. *Joe Anthony, U.S. Marine Corps, 1969.*

Infantry training, Fort Benning, Georgia. "Hurry up and wait." *Al Stewart, U.S. Army, 1970.*

Since I was not a part of this particular unit, I don't know exactly what they were doing, but I would suspect they had received orders for a certain location that they had located enemy. That would be a very large artillery round that they're firing. I was just fascinated with this; it was just beautiful. I grew up in Greenville, Mississippi, and I almost never left there. Suddenly I was in the army, halfway around the world. It was a very exciting period for me. *Gerald Harrison, U.S. Army, 1970.*

You're screeching down this river full bore back to your base camp, and you're far enough out on this river you're relatively safe. You can say, *Man, this guy's having a good time.* He's happy, coming in off a night patrol. But a little background on that. I'm sitting in this gun tub. I'm a front gunner. These gun turrets on these things kind of just swing around. They would hold probably 2,000 or 2,500 shells. There were times when the gun barrels were melting. I don't really like to think of myself being behind that. Coming back from Vietnam, I've never, ever, ever, ever been able to hold a weapon or hunt. I'm glad that that picture was taken, but it's got kind of those mixed feelings about it. *David Prevette, U.S. Navy, 1968.*

This is a typical scene you would see along the roadside between Phu Bai and Da Nang—a young Vietnamese farmer riding on the back of a water buffalo. Water buffalo in Vietnam were extremely high-valued animals, and individuals who had water buffalos were considered to be very wealthy in Vietnam. These animals would have been used to pull plows in rice farming. *Gerald Harrison, U.S. Army, 1970.*

Above A group of guys that met at the Da Nang hospital talking about the world. And wondering if we would ever see it again. *Ayman Fareed, U.S. Marine Corps, 1968.*

Opposite, top This little girl's name was Hue. She lived in a small village near our LZ where we had an information network set up to trace enemy movement. *Carl Galie Jr., U.S. Army, 1968.*

Opposite, bottom It was right after mail call. This isn't even my newspaper. Everybody read everybody's everything. You could not get enough stuff to read. I'm a reader, so I would read my letters, and if you'd let me, I'd read your letters and I'd let you read my letters. Some people sent hometown newspapers, and we were starved for that because everything we got was so filtered. The military had their own little *Stars and Stripes* newspaper, but looking back, you know, we didn't get any news. *Larry Dishon, U.S. Army, 1970.*

I think it was Christmas of '67. We were guarding a bridge near Duc Pho, and it was kind of like a two-week break when you come in and guard a bridge after being out in the boonies. That was a young kid out of the village there. He was probably eight, nine, ten, full of energy. He'd come up and we'd give him food or rations or whatever we had. We took to being friends with him. When something was going to happen, he would come and stay with us. And nothing would happen to our bridge, but other bridges down the road would be booby-trapped. It was a surprise to see him standing there when I looked at this picture again. *Dale Doub, U.S. Army, 1967.*

Above This particular picture is a guy with whom I shared a cube in our barracks. His name was Jim Coleman. The poster was Jim's. Someone that he knew—I don't know if it was a family member—sent it to him. We were young, and we thought of the irony of it, and we were being smart asses, is what we were doing. It's exactly what we were doing. Of course, we always stood the chance of having someone come through on an I.G. inspection and telling us to take it down. But that was just reminiscent of the time. *Truett Chadwick Jr., U.S. Air Force, 1970.*

Right We're more than likely on a ridgeline here, over watching a valley, a trail or a river from an observation point in the jungle. There's a second person over here, and by blowing it [the snapshot] up, I can see an ear there and the top of his head, and I think that's Richard Jarbowski, but there's no way I can swear to that. But I didn't know that second person existed. I'm right proud of the fact that I wasn't able to see the second guy, and I wasn't able to see the poncho liner at all in that very small photograph. It makes me feel like our training and our effort of being in a stealth mode, so to speak, was working real well. *Al Stewart, U.S. Army, 1971.*

This is a scene where the tide is out, and it's dropped 10 to 15 feet. This is a very silty mud, and when it's out we have to climb up this mud. The guy touching the weeds is trying to stabilize himself, getting ready to take the next step. This guy on the far right is just taking one step in order to pull up his back leg in order to take another step. Because when you step down, you sink with your leading leg. You pretty much sink to your pelvis, and the more weight you have on you, the more you sink down. *Robert Karraker, U.S. Army, 1969.*

Photo submitted by Bart Near in
memory of his father, Sergeant Major
(Ret.) E.G. Near, now deceased.
Sergeant Major Near served five tours in
Vietnam in MACV/SOG. E.G. Near, U.S.
Army, 1962–71.

This is team Frankfurt returning from a mission. There's nothing like coming back and coming back whole, not hurt, and being able to get out of those clothes. You don't even take your shoes off the whole time you're out there, so you're filthy. Clem (*in front*) is intense, and that's him on the way *out*. You ought to see him on the way in; his eyes will burn a hole through you. Clem was the most intense soldier I ever knew. I didn't particularly like him because he was so strict, but I knew that he was the best and if I could do like he did, I had a much better chance of surviving. Later on, we became great friends. *Al Stewart, U.S. Army, 1971.*

These heavy clouds in the background were B-52 strikes. You never saw the planes; they're probably up 30,000 feet. After this, these PBRs (patrol boat rivers) and various other landing craft put the Army people on shore. At this point, they're putting in those troops on this hard ground. In '66, the powers that be in the Navy decided to use these small boats up in these rivers and canals. The last time it was used was in the Civil War, when they used these little amphibious craft. *David Prevette, U.S. Navy, 1969.*

Above   I could smell bacon, and I could hear it. We were all within a small compound on top of a hill. We were just kind of teasing each other, and they were down in here doing this. And I saw them cooking, and they were cooking breakfast, and I thought, *Wow, they've got real food.* And we're up there, you know, eating C-rations and trading bananas from the local Vietnamese. But we weren't force recon—I was with an artillery group—and we weren't getting invited in. *Dustin Simmons, U.S. Marine Corps, 1966.*

Opposite, top   A U.S. Air Force F-100 Super Sabre firing rockets over South Vietnam. Robert Garry was stationed at Ton Son Nut Air Base with the 377th Squadron. *Robert Garry, U.S. Air Force, 1968.*

Opposite, bottom   Being in a hospital unit, I saw a lot of good things that we did for the Vietnamese people. This photo was taken in Can Tho in February 1968. *Don McClenny, U.S. Army, 1968.*

As a part of the preventive medicine unit, we did goodwill type of activities for the local Vietnamese kids. We routinely, once or twice a week, would visit the local orphanages. We would go in and basically have little training sessions where we'd show the kids how to brush their teeth, and we'd give them a brush and toothpaste and just teach them to wash their hands and various things like that. It was kind of heart jerking work, but actually, really, some of the most rewarding things that we did. It made you feel good after you left. There were a lot of kids there. *Gerald Harrison, U.S. Army, 1971.*

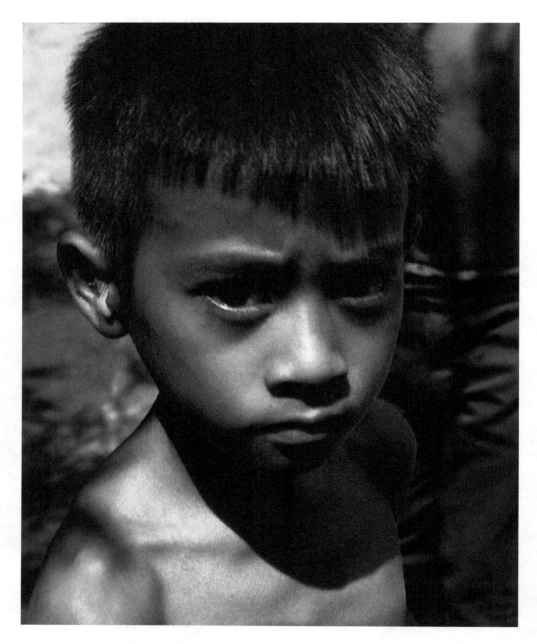

This is a picture of one of the kids in the city of Hue, near one of the ice plants that we went in and inspected. They all knew that when we came in, we brought gum and candy and would throw it out at them, and this is a typical little kid that you would see clamoring around the jeeps, waiting for a handout. They were dirt poor. They had nothing to their name. *Gerald Harrison, U.S. Army, 1970.*

We were right close to Bien Hoa Air Base because we were supporting the 173rd Airborne. The Airborne lieutenant come by there and said, "Boys, there might be some enemy fire tonight, you'll need to dig in." I think to myself, well, I'm going to dig me a big one while I'm into it. I'm probably on my knees right there. You didn't dig no deeper than you really had to. The dang ground's hard. If it wasn't monsoon, you really couldn't dig. That was a good digging place. *Andy West, U.S. Army, 1966.*

We were in a pretty good-sized village, down in the Third Corps, part of the Mekong Delta. We had literally walked into this village out of the rice paddies early that morning, and we started taking fire from a sniper. He kept about 100 people at bay for four hours. Normally we would just call helicopters and have them help us and burn up the general area and hope we can kill whatever was sniping at us. In this situation we couldn't, because there were civilians and you just can't shoot up a village. I finally got a Cab unit that was in the area that was willing to send over these little APCs and a couple of tanks just to get us out of there. I took the photograph to celebrate their arrival. That was the first time I'd stood up in four hours. *Larry Dishon, U.S. Army, 1970.*

We had been in general quarters for about three hours, and without anyone calling in fires, I got bored and thought I would sneak out of my duty station and climb on top of the super structure and wait until the fire was called again. I was up 75 feet. I was up pretty high. I might have been up there ten minutes and I heard the buzzers start to go off. It was a three-second buzzer, and on the third buzzer, they would fire. This flash here lasts only for a split second, and this one caught it just right. It shows the awesome power of the ship itself. The shell that went out was probably about four feet tall and eight inches around, so it was quite a shell. It weighed 1,500 pounds. It's like shooting a Cadillac out of the end of one of these things. It was tremendously loud. I could feel the heat. *Barry Whitley, U.S. Navy, 1967.*

Opposite This guy sitting here is a door gunner, covering the observation helicopter as it turns away from wherever the action is. He's having a ball. He gets to shoot all he wants. On this particular day, we were on canal duty, near the Iron Triangle in the war zone, Three Corps, and we got to do a lot of shooting. It was fun. It was a gorgeous day. Every day in Vietnam was pretty, and this was just another pretty day. When I went to Vietnam, I was 29 years old. I was a semiprofessional soldier. I had no problems with going. *Bill Abbey, U.S. Army, 1969.*

This was up close to a place called Wonder Beach. The sand was white, just white. The sand reflected up the heat, and this was the middle of the day. You see how my dog had his tongue hung out. He was close to passing out. I said, "I can't walk him anymore," so we got on a track vehicle, and it's got 106mm recoilless rifles on it. My dog was one of the first dogs in Vietnam. His name was Mutsu. He would not walk into anything. If it was there, he'd let you know. He was good with personnel. He could find caches of ammo, food, and he was good with mines. When it was time to eat, he'd always get the first spoonful of C-rations. The reason I am here today is because of him. *Joe Anthony, U.S. Marine Corps, 1968.*

That was sort of the lull before the storm. The infantry, the grunts, they were up here on the other side of this ridge and were in one heck of a firefight, and we were just waiting to shoot. We're in the artillery. We're there for fire support and we're waiting for our coordinates. You can see we're not loaded. You know, a firefight is a pretty common thing. You've got to realize, we were crazy. We were only 18 years old, and we had very little common sense. An Army man once told me that he'd never met a Marine that thought he was going to die. *Ron Shouse, U.S. Marine Corps, 1967.*

This guy, his nickname was "Tiny." He was probably six-three, six-four, something like that. That's an M-60 machine gun that he's carrying. It's probably a 26-pound weapon and that's his loader back behind him, chasing him with the ammo box. We were actually under fire when this was taken. I was actually standing up when that photograph was taken. Most the time my favorite position was as close to Mother Earth as I could get. *Mike Callahan, U.S. Army, 1970.*

Somebody ran out of luck here. This is north of Chu Lai, a couple of Viet Cong got caught. Probably man and wife, probably about twenty, twenty-five. They were being taken back for interrogation. I don't know if they had their shoes taken off of them or not; they might have lost their shoes trying to escape or hide. I wasn't involved in the capture; I just happen to be sitting on the truck there, and they came by and I just took a picture. We didn't capture many at all. *Dustin Simmons, U.S. Marine Corps, 1966.*

This is the aftermath of the opening fight with that NVA unit. We fought 'em off and on for three days. It wasn't hard contact every minute of the day. But we got an armor unit in there, and you can see one of their tracks in the back. It's an armored personnel carrier, APCs is what we called 'em for short, or that and "Rolling Reynolds Wrap" 'cause bullets could go right through them. That fellow, as I recall he caught a bullet in the tip of his nose, and it grazed his cheek, so it wasn't a life-threatening wound. It upset him, though. *Mike Callahan, U.S. Army, 1970.*

What had happened was that we'd supplied on the afternoon of the sixth of February, and the next day, we was needing to get the water cans back out, so the command chopper thought he could just come pick the water cans back up and leave, and they shot the pilot when he came in. So, we received fire, and we was pinned down there the night before and all the next day. The other chopper that you see the tail section of is a dust off. When he started to land, they hit the tail rudder and the chopper started doing a 360 inside the perimeter there. Finally, they called in F-4s that afternoon. They're probably popping smoke there for the perimeter for the F-4s or the Cobras so they'll know where you're at. War's a funny thing. What may seem like a bad moment to you is, after the firefight, a real peaceful moment because you're just kind of kicking back. That was probably during a lull when you just pull your camera out and take a picture of something that you probably try to remember. *Dale Doub, U.S. Army, 1968.*

Opposite I was stationed with the Third MPs, right outside of Da Nang. This was just doing some laundry. Basically, you get your bucket of water and you wet your pants down and lay it on this board. You get some soap on there and scrub your pants. I had maybe five, six pair of pants, and this pair I have on was the only pair I had that was clean at the time, or cleaner than the rest of them. The next day, if you were still in the area that long, you would wash the other pair. *Joe Anthony, U.S. Marine Corps, 1968.*

I was a radio operator for a company of about 200 men, and this is probably 25 or 28 days out in the field with no shower; 100 degrees during the day, 80 degrees at night. So what I would do is I would get on the radio and call artillery and just say, "Can you make about six holes in the ground for us right out there?" Where we were, this old rice paddy, would take maybe an hour for that to fill up with water, it would just seep in and it would be kind of clean. It was seeping in through the sand after the explosion in the ground, so we would just wait, lay back, go out and we had six nice little bathing holes. *Larry Dishon, U.S. Army, 1970.*

Long Bien. We were transferring from one evacuation hospital to another. Being in a hospital unit, I saw a lot of good things that we did for the Vietnamese people. *Don McClenny, U.S. Army, 1968.*

Agony. Agony of war…desperation. This is not the thing that the military or the media would really publish. *Robert Karraker, U.S. Army, 1969.*

Opposite The USO had sponsored an outing for military personnel at Cam Ranh Bay. Cam Ranh was an in-country R&R location, so I managed to wangle a spot on this boat. As we floated out into this lagoon, the local fishermen came paddling out. What they wanted was to get their picture taken and get beer. We'd toss them a beer, and they'd let us take their picture. What amazed me about that area, especially the lagoon where we were, was the clarity of the water, and the blue. It was a relaxing day to sort of forget and try to have pleasant memories of home and remove yourself from the situation at hand. *Truett Chadwick Jr., U.S. Air Force, 1970.*

Vietnamese children with soldiers during a supply convoy stop. *Ralph Lee, U.S. Army, 1966.*

Opposite This is me and Xinh Mai, a resident of the orphanage at An Lac. Betty Tisdale and Madame Vu Thi Ngai operated it, and in the closing days of the war, they organized Operation Baby Lift. Little Xinh Mai had to be left behind. Today, she owns a small clothing store in Ho Chi Minh City and has two daughters, one a physician, the other a merchandise manager with a department store. *Mike Callahan, U.S. Army, 1970.*

I knew the soldiers being airlifted out. They were with the 2nd Battalion of the 28th Infantry regiment. I used to go out with that unit quite a bit. *Mike Callahan, U.S. Army, 1970.*

Opposite A GI with Ngoc at the An Lac Orphanage. Ngoc made it out during Operation Baby Lift and was adopted by Kathy Kreider of Hershey, Pennsylvania. She lived a full life and had many friends. I spoke briefly at her funeral last year. *Mike Callahan, U.S. Army, 1970.*

This photo was taken of the main line of resistance. There was an enemy force out there, and the two gentlemen standing are General Herbert E. Wolff (*left*) and his aide-de-camp, Captain Mike Sarff. General Wolff and Mike Sarff have both passed away. I attended both funerals. *Mike Callahan, U.S. Army, 1970.*

This VC was taken prisoner, and that was very rare. I think he was left back to maintain a tunnel complex we found in the area. Notice how the Agent Orange worked. Our area of operation was heavily defoliated. *Mike Callahan, U.S. Army, 1970.*

We were receiving sniper fire. The M-79 grenadier was looking for a muzzle flash as "base runners" ran toward where they suspected the sniper would be. The "runners" were out to draw fire, and the grenadier would, hopefully, eliminate the threat. *Mike Callahan, U.S. Army, 1970.*

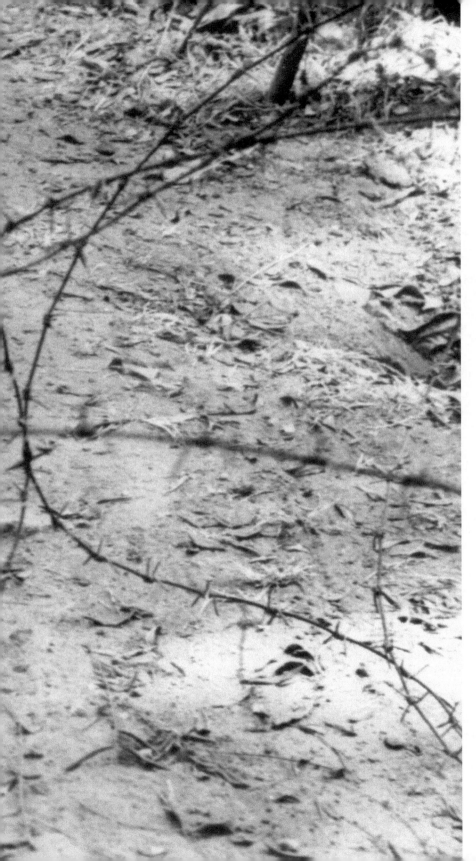

The toddler. We went into a village we suspected was hostile, and he was the only living soul we found. We could see people across a paddy complex, and they were sure watching us. We left the baby alone and left the village in a different direction from the way we'd come. The people watching us were women and older men. No young men. *Mike Callahan, U.S. Army, 1970.*

Above General Herbert E. Wolff presented this young sniper with a Bronze Star. He killed five hard-core VC who terrorized a village repetitively. They would go in the village at night and have their way with the women. *Mike Callahan, U.S. Army, 1970.*

Opposite, top These 122mm Soviet Katyusha rockets were found near Lai Khe around Christmas 1969. Lai Khe was nicknamed "Rocket City" because of so many attacks. *Mike Callahan, U.S. Army, 1970.*

Opposite, bottom One VC sapper killed, the other was captured. They tried to get through our wire at Fire Support Base Colorado, near Vung Tau. *Mike Callahan, U.S. Army, 1970.*

Above Results of a bomb strike. *Mike Callahan, U.S. Army, 1970.*

Opposite, top We found a base camp. The tunnel complex was huge, and the officers had flame-throwers brought in. They'd fire a "wet shot" into a vent or entrance and then drop a grenade in. You can see the flame-thrower tanks on the soldier's back. *Mike Callahan, U.S. Army, 1970.*

Opposite, bottom A temporary battalion headquarters while they were constructing Fire Support Base Colorado. Note the "floor" is comprised of mortar ammo boxes. *Mike Callahan, U.S. Army, 1970.*

Above Our "limo" driver telling us that our trip to the jungle is nearly complete. *Al Stewart, U.S. Army, 1970.*

Right Golf Company Rangers Frank Svensson and Mike Moorehead sunbathing on Christmas Day in Da Nang. *Al Stewart, U.S. Army, 1970.*

Above A U.S. Army base camp near Ben Hoa, 1966. *Andy West, U.S. Army, 1966.*

Opposite, top Team Moscow, G Company Rangers, Da Nang. That's my CAR-15 modified with a 40mm grenade launcher. *Al Stewart, U.S. Army, 1970.*

Opposite, bottom A helicopter crew shot this tiger and brought it back to camp. *Bill Abbey, U.S. Army, 1969–70.*

Soldiers practice firing on the side of Vung Ro Mountain. *Barry Chatillion, U.S. Army, 1968.*

Phu Loi, the Iron Triangle. I served two tours as a pilot and aviation commander on the UHIC gunship. *Bill Abbey, U.S. Army, 1966.*

We're passing time at a remote communications site on Vung Ro Mountain. I retired as a sergeant major in the Army after 30 years. *Barry Chatillion, U.S. Army, 1968.*

Casualty removal near Tan Son Nhut Air Force base. *Robert Garry, U.S. Air Force, 1968.*

Opposite 9th Division engineers checking for road mines before traffic is opened in the morning. *Robert Karraker, U.S. Army, 1969.*

A forward observer with the 9th Division's 2nd Battalion, 60th Infantry, calls in adjustment figures to the Tan Tru fire base for an artillery barrage. The artillery is often used to soften up an area before the infantrymen move in to sear and clear. *Robert Karraker, U.S. Army, 1969.*

Opposite   A sampan full of Vietnamese desiring medical treatment arrives at the site of a MEDCAP held by the 2nd Battalion, 60th Infantry, near their Tan Tru base camp. 9th Division units held MEDCAPS constantly to bring modern medical treatment to countless hamlets and villages in the Mekong Delta. *Robert Karraker, U.S. Army, 1968.*

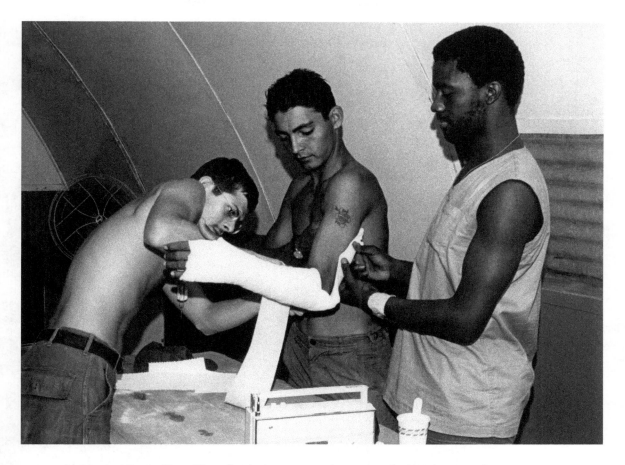

9th Med at Dong Tam. Their facilities may not have equaled Walter Reed Army
Hospital, but when it came to treating wounded or sick "old reliable soldiers," they
had the equipment and doctors to do the job very adequately. *Robert Karraker, U.S.
Army, 1969.*

Opposite   9th Division—this was the 100,000 105mm artillery round getting ready to
be fired. *Robert Karraker, U.S. Army, 1968.*

After they had been on patrol for an extended time, a swift boat comes alongside for supplies. *Barry Whitley, U.S. Navy, 1967.*

Above   Taking a break after carrying that 26-pound M-60! *Dale Doub, U.S. Army, 1968.*

Opposite, top   Damage after a mission. I was with the 8th Bomber Squadron. *Dave Eckrote, U.S. Air Force, 1966.*

Opposite, bottom   That's me on the back of a "3/4" with the M-60. We were on a convoy headed to Dak To. *Danny Howard, U.S. Army, 1968.*

Red Cross checking on the troops in the field. *Dale Doub, U.S. Army, 1968.*

On a day patrol on the Ham Luong River, we searched a junk and found ammo and supplies. There was no resistance, so we put them on board. However, we received small-arms fire from the Viet Cong as we were leaving the search area. A crewmember was shot in the arm and would recover. In this photo we are almost to our base at My Tho. *David Prevette, U.S. Navy, 1969.*

It is, if I remember correctly, along the perimeter of the base that I was at in Phu Bai. What these vehicles do is they are lined up along the perimeter, and if there is any report of enemy along the outside of the perimeter, they would simply open up and essentially level that particular quadrant of the firebase area. The idea is that if there's any enemy there, there will not be any left after that exercise. These were commonly referred to as a "mad minute." A very, very interesting event to witness. I felt fairly secure at night. *Gerald Harrison, U.S. Army, 1970.*

On June 17, 1969, while patrolling on Long Tau River, we were ambushed on a small canal at 0230 hours. Our PBR was hit by small-arms fire and 57mm rockets. Our cover boat had one KIA and two wounded. As we turned back toward them with my .50 cal wide open, suddenly my gun tub was violently hit and I was almost knocked out of it. Then we rejoined our cover boat 121 and were full speed out of the canal and heading back to Nha Be. After a long patrol and tying up at the pier, I headed to the chow hall and then had a few hours' sleep. I was awakened and told to come back to the piers…what awaited me would stab my heart and bring me to my knees. I saw a large hole on the left side of my gun tub and then realized an unexploded 57mm rocket grenade had fired into my gun tub…an unexploded weapon of death! I held it and thanked God! I was back on the river soon. *David Prevette, U.S. Navy, 1969.*

Looking down from atop the Saigon Hotel at the hustle and bustle below. Saigon was a transit site for troops awaiting orders. *David Prevette, U.S. Navy, 1969.*

Hill 54, Chu Lai during the monsoon season. Even in the rain the captain's mighty-mite had to be cleaned. *Dustin Simmons, U.S. Marine Corps, 1966.*

Practicing on the .50 cal. *Dustin Simmons, U.S. Marine Corps, 1966.*

131

Opposite Two Vietnamese monks in Da Nang. *Gerald Harrison, U.S. Army, 1970.*

Below Aboard the USS *Point Defiance*. It took 21 days to sail from Vietnam to Camp Del Mar, California. *Ernest Lesaine, U.S. Marine Corps, 1970.*

One of the royal entry gates to the provincial grounds of the capital city of Hue. This was a major battleground in 1968 Tet Offensive. War damage was evident on the walls. You could enter and observe the smoky prayer rooms, but you had to first remove your boots and weapons. *Gerald Harrison, U.S. Army, 1970.*

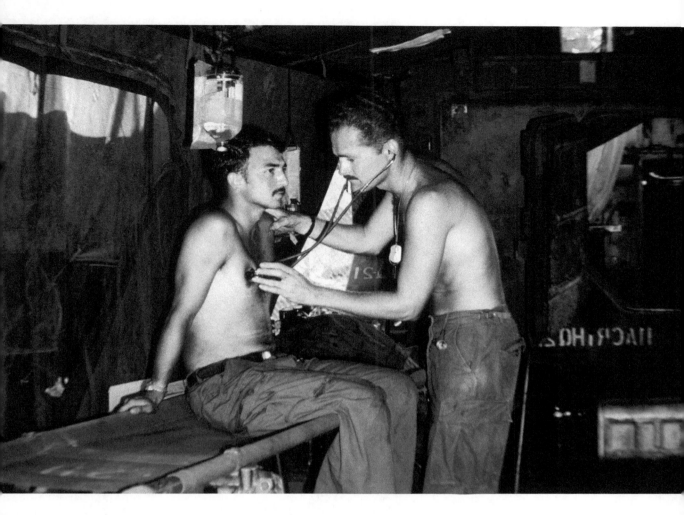

Above Doc Revinger with the 85th Evac Hospital in Phu Bai. A routine medical checkup. *Gerald Harrison, U.S. Army, 1970.*

Opposite, top Soldiers with their cameras on R&R. The person on the far left is a veterinarian attached to a vet clinic in Phu Bai. The next person is a doctor with the 85th Evac Hospital. *Gerald Harrison, U.S. Army, 1970.*

Opposite, bottom This is me and a fellow officer near Da Nang on a South China Sea beach. Two men and myself would drive in a 2½-ton truck from Phu Bai to Da Nang over the Hai Van Pass to attend a monthly meeting. *Gerald Harrison, U.S. Army, 1970.*

Vietnamese children herding ducks on the Perfume River. *Gerald Harrison, U.S. Army, 1970.*

Opposite Vietnamese family living in the ravages of war. This was taken on the banks of the Perfume River between Phu Bai and Hue. We referred to this river as Sampan Alley. *Gerald Harrison, U.S. Army, 1970.*

I would participate with dentists and doctors from the 85th Evac Hospital to periodically visit and give medical checkups and care to children in the orphanages. We did this primarily in Hue. *Gerald Harrison, U.S. Army, 1970.*

142

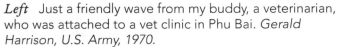

Left Just a friendly wave from my buddy, a veterinarian, who was attached to a vet clinic in Phu Bai. *Gerald Harrison, U.S. Army, 1970.*

Above "Wounded in Action, 17 Dec '70." Occurred on one of our monthly staff meeting trips over the Hai Van Pass en route from Phu Bai to DeNang. A sniper aimed a little too low, and the round hit the door that thankfully stopped its passage. A soldier in my unit awarded the truck a "Purple Heart." *Gerald Harrison, U.S. Army, 1970.*

On patrol—looking for
"Charlie." *Joe Anthony, U.S.
Marine Corps, 1968.*

Early U.S. Navy "brown water" gunboat. Harry Reich, U.S. Navy, 1965–70.

That's me on the My Tho River in a monsoon. We were coming back from the Dong Tam Base Camp. I served six-month tours from 1965 to 1970 with Boat Support Unit 1 and UDT/SEAL Teams One and Two. *Harry Reich, U.S. Navy, 1965–70.*

Me and my scout dog, Mutsu, waiting for a chopper. We didn't have any idea where we were going. *Joe Anthony, U.S. Marine Corps, 1968.*

Scout dog training at 3rd MP Battalion outside Da Nang. *Joe Anthony, U.S. Marine Corps, 1968.*

Taking a break on patrol, 1968, near Hue (Tet Offensive). *Joe Anthony, U.S. Marine Corps, 1968.*

Opposite, top   Setting up on a hilltop. *Joe Anthony, U.S. Marine Corps, 1968.*

Opposite, bottom   "The place of angels"—that's what they called it. *Joe Anthony, U.S. Marine Corps, 1968.*

Below   Me and my scout dog getting ready to go on patrol. *Joe Anthony, U.S. Marine Corps, 1968.*

Patrolling on Wonder Beach. *Joe Anthony, U.S. Marine Corps, 1968.*

Coming out of a patrol in the mountains. *Joe Anthony, U.S. Marine Corps, 1968.*

Scout dog brothers. Taken in August 1968 at the rock pile right before my dog got hit. He was medivac'd out, went into surgery to remove shrapnel and recovered. *Joe Anthony, U.S. Marine Corps, 1968.*

Opposite Always had my camera close. My camera was an Olympus PEN-F. It shot a 35mm half frame. *Joe Anthony, U.S. Marine Corps, 1968.*

Propaganda poster—we'd find them everywhere. *Joe Anthony, U.S. Marine Corps, 1968.*

Opposite My friend Raymond Smith, shaving in the field. *Larry Kirby, U.S. Army, 1969.*

Above A fellow soldier with his pet monkey. North of the Mekong Delta. *John Cashion, U.S. Air Force, 1968.*

Opposite, top Lark landing craft on the coast. *Joe Anthony, U.S. Marine Corps, 1968.*

Opposite, bottom Me and Bobby Shepard, my childhood friend. We grew up three doors apart in Winston-Salem and reconnected on the DMZ in Vietnam! *Joe Anthony, U.S. Marine Corps, 1968.*

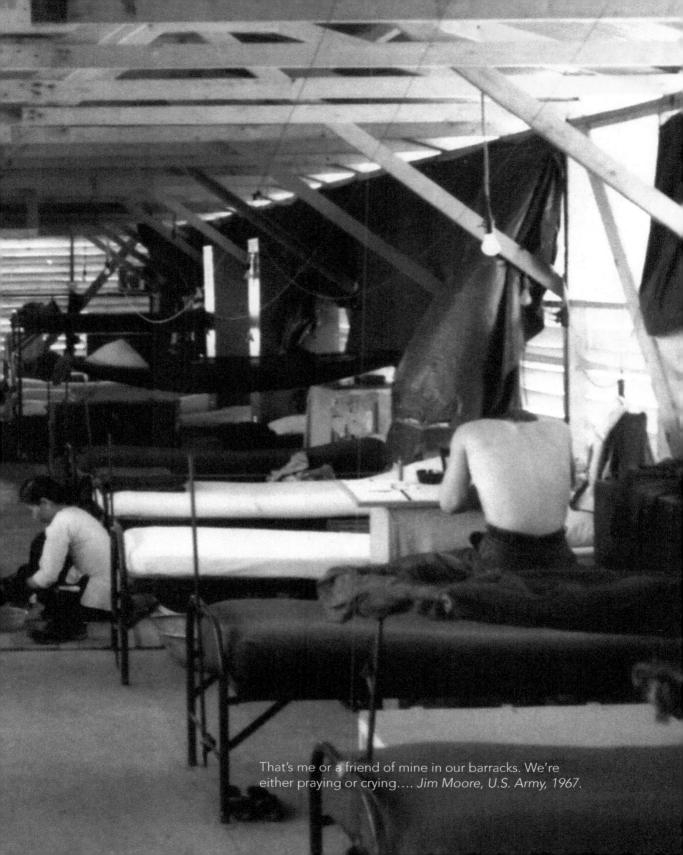

That's me or a friend of mine in our barracks. We're either praying or crying.... *Jim Moore, U.S. Army, 1967.*

Opposite, top   Two of my best friends are in this picture. I had heard the Vietnamese people sometimes had dogs as meals, and I didn't want that to happen to these two. *Jim Moore, U.S. Army, 1967.*

Opposite, bottom   American singer Anita Bryant with a soldier at Bob Hope's USO Christmas Show. Tent City, outside Nha Trang. *Robert Crutchfield, U.S. Army, 1966.*

Below   U.S. Army convoy headed to Pleiku. *Ralph Lee, U.S. Army, 1966.*

Montanyards gather
to watch my truck
convoy. We transported
supplies to the Central
Highlands. *Ralph Lee,
U.S. Army, 1966.*

A supply convoy on the way to the Central Highlands. *Ralph Lee, U.S. Army, 1966.*

Above Mid-day heat, South Vietnam. *Ralph Lee, U.S. Army, 1966.*

Right The Red Cross offered a "cruise" one Sunday afternoon that went around the area of Cam Ranh Bay. I was able to see where the French had placed machine gun nests in the early '50s. For history buffs, the trip was really interesting. *Truett Chadwick Jr., U.S. Air Force, 1969.*

R&R at Cam Ranh Bay. *Truett Chadwick Jr., U.S. Air Force, 1969.*

You're thinking about your family, what's going on with them. You're putting your thoughts together, and you're trying not to tell them too much about what's going on to worry them. My wife says I was writing home to her. This had to be in the first part of '68 because that was when I was carrying a gun. I guess I was a pretty good-sized boy, and they put that ol' 26-pound gun on you and I carried it. M-60 is *the* gun. If it's working, it's a pretty sound. But when that thing clicks one time, you think the world has ended. *Dale Doub, U.S. Army, 1968.*

This is the sign over the door in the hooch where I lived. I had a relatively small amount of time left in country before I was going to fly out of that place, and the common term when you had little time left in country was to say that you were "short." So I memorialized that by making a sign and hanging it over my door just to remind myself every morning that I was "short." *Gerald Harrison, U.S. Army, 1971.*

We just heard we were headed home! *Ernest Lesaine, U.S. Marine Corps, 1970.*

The sign every soldier wanted to see.
Larry Dishon, U.S. Army, 1971.

The filing time shown in the date line on domestic telegrams is LOCAL TIME at point of origin. Time of receipt is LOCAL TIME at point of destination

1011P EDT JUN 10 68 AA394

AA A WA306 XV GOVT PDB 2 EXTRA WASHINGTON DC 10 746P EDT

MR AND MRS WILLIAM E WATKINS SR, DONT PHONE

2809 ROSEMARY DRIVE WINSTON SALEM NCAR

THIS IS TO CONFIRM THAT YOUR SON CORPORAL LARRY J WATKINS USMC
WAS INJURED ON 5 JUNE 1968 IN THE VICINITY OF QUANG NAM, REPUBLIC
OF VIETNAM. HE SUSTAINED FRAGMENTATION WOUNDS TO THE RIGHT
SIDE OF THE BACK FROM HOSTILE MORTAR FIRE WHILE ON AN OPERATION.
HIS CONDITION AND PROGNOSIS WERE BOTH GOOD. HE IS PRESENTLY
RECEIVING TREATMENT AT THE STATION HOSPITAL DANANG. YOUR ANXIETY
IS REALIZED AND YOU ARE ASSURED THAT HE IS RECEIVING THE BEST
OF CARE. IT IS HOPED THAT HE WILL COMMUNICATE WITH YOU SOON
INFORMING YOU OF HIS WELFARE. HIS MAILING ADDRESS REMAINS THE
SAME

LEONARD F CHAPMAN JR GENERAL USMC COMMANDER OF THE MARINE
CORPS

SF1201(R2-65)

A telegram sent to Larry Watkins's parents after he was wounded in action. Mr. Watkins received two Purple Heart awards in Vietnam. He later changed his name to Ayman Fareed. Ayman Fareed, U.S. Marine Corps, 1968.

NHA-TRANG, 4 MARCH 1967

Dear Robert E. Crutchfield,

As soon as I received your letter and two pictures I am doing my best to write for you. I thank you for both. Mr Elkins remove the 2-3-67, he has a order-mission in operation two months. He talks to me: it is dangerous! I have wanted to write for you but I have lost your address. Excuse-me

I am glad to hear you meet your wife and your family. This day my wife goes to Qui-Nhơn, to visit my father-in-law. She is not yet come back. I stay alone with my children. When I go to work all the night, my baby-sons sleep with my house-girl.

I read your letter and explain for my children, sometimes, they see a MP, who transit in our street, they call Bob (your name). They talk to me: you will to send plaything, please because they have beaucoup Gum now. As baby LAN and HƯƠNG, they send two pictures and they ask you to send two conicals.

Five Americans live my house, two Negros Mr Dodson who live your room in my house. Sometimes he helps me to learn English. My family is well now. Thank GOD. You talk to your wife Hello for me.

I hope you receive this letter and you will to write for me.

Love
Lanh

NGUYỄN-VĂN-LÃNH

Letter from a Vietnamese father to a U.S. soldier. He had befriended the family during his tour. Robert Crutchfield, U.S. Army, MP (Military Police), 1966.

I worked in a hospital over there. For the troops, this was probably the best sign in Vietnam. *Don McClenny, U.S. Army, 1967.*

Opposite North Carolina Vietnam vets with a UHIH Huey helicopter. Photo by Martin Tucker.

APRIL 2003

I hope you've enjoyed this look into my past. I guess it shows a side of me you didn't or couldn't know. One day, perhaps, your son or daughter might want to know what grandpa did in Vietnam and you can show them. For sure, I did other things there, some tedious, some terrible. This accounting is what I choose to remember and it is how I would like to be remembered. I believe it is up to us to find the good in everything. Sometimes it is easy and sometimes not... but it's always there.

Dad

Last page from the photo album assembled by Mike Callahan, North Carolina Vietnam veteran, for his daughter.

ABOUT THE AUTHOR

MARTIN TUCKER IS AN AWARD-WINNING photojournalist, documentary filmmaker and speaker. He was a photographer for the *Pacific Palisades Post*, the *Malibu Times*, the *Winston-Salem Journal, American Profile Magazine, Community Arts Café* magazine and *Southern California Sports* magazine. His work has been published in the *Los Angeles Times*, the *Washington Post*, the *New York Post*, *Charlotte* magazine, the Associated Press, *Our State: The Magazine of North Carolina*, *Humanities* magazine, *Vietnam Veterans of America* magazine, *US Weekly* and *People* magazine. His documentary work includes *Patty: This Is My Normal*, a documentary short film selection at the RiverRun International Film Festival; *The World War II Veterans Project*, interviews with and portraits of more than one hundred World War II veterans; and *5-25-06: Rolling Thunder Rides to Washington*. He received the Distinguished Service Award from the Military Order of the Purple Heart for creating and curating the exhibition "A Thousand Words: Photographs by Vietnam Veterans." Martin was also chosen as one of the 20 People of the Year by *GoTriad* magazine for this exhibit. He is a former photography and computer graphics coordinator and instructor at the Sawtooth School for Visual Art in Winston-Salem, North Carolina, and currently teaches photography and digital media at Summit School in Winston-Salem, North Carolina. He served in the U.S. Navy from 1967 to 1969.

CPSIA information can be obtained
at www.ICGtesting.com
Printed in the USA
BVHW050738090222
628491BV00003B/361